Apréndete tus números/Know Your Numbers

Huevos y patas
Cuenta de dos en dos

Eggs and Legs
Counting by Twos

por/by Michael Dahl

ilustrado por/illustrated by Todd Ouren

traducción/translation: Dr. Martín Luis Guzmán Ferrer

PICTURE WINDOW BOOKS
a capstone imprint

Special thanks to our advisers for their expertise:
Stuart Farm, M.Ed., Mathematic Lecturer
University of North Dakota, Grand Forks

Susan Kesselring, M.A., Literacy Educator
Rosemount-Apple Valley-Eagan (Minnesota) School District

Editor: Christianne Jones
Spanish Copy Editor: Adálin Torres-Zayas
Designer: Todd Ouren
Book Designer: Eric Manske
Production Specialist: Jane Klenk
The illustrations in this book were prepared digitally.

Picture Window Books
151 Good Counsel Drive
P.O. Box 669
Mankato, MN 56002-0669
877-845-8392
www.capstonepub.com

All books published by Picture Window Books
are manufactured with paper containing at least
10 percent post-consumer waste.

Library of Congress Cataloging-in-Publication Data
Dahl, Michael.
     [Huevos y patas. English & Spanish]
     Huevos y patas : cuenta de dos en dos / por Michael Dahl =
Eggs and legs : counting by twos / by Michael Dahl
     p. cm. –(Apréndete tus números = Know your numbers)
     Summary: "Introduces counting by twos by counting the
number of legs coming out of eggs. Readers are invited to find
hidden numbers on an illustrated activity page–in both English
and Spanish"–Provided by publisher.
     ISBN 978-1-4048-6296-8 (library binding)
     1. Counting–Juvenile literature. 2. Multiplication–Juvenile
literature. I. Title. II. Title: Eggs and legs.
QA113.D32818 2011
513.2'11–dc22   2010009875

Printed in the United States of America in North Mankato, Minnesota.
042011   006178R

2

Mrs. Hen stared at her empty nest.

La Sra. Gallina se quedó viendo su nido vacío.

"Oh no!" she cried.
"Where have all
my eggs gone?"

"¡Huy no!" exclamó.
"¿A dónde se han ido
todos mis huevos?"

3

4

TWO little legs went running into the barn.

DOS patitas entraron corriendo al establo.

FOUR little legs were
hiding in the corn.

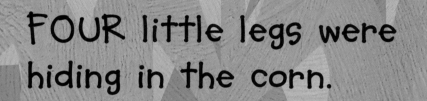

CUATRO patitas se
escondieron en el maizal.

6

7

SIX little legs were
chasing the dog.

2 4 6

SEIS patitas
perseguían al perro.

9

EIGHT little legs were
bothering a cow.

OCHO patitas molestaban
a la vaca.

10

11

TEN little legs were climbing
on the tractor.

DIEZ patitas se
trepaban al tractor.

TWELVE little legs were playing with the pig.

2 4 6 8 10 12

14

DOCE patitas estaban
jugando con el cerdo.

FOURTEEN little legs were scurrying through the beans.

2 4 6 8 10 12 14

CATORCE patitas correteaban entre los frijoles.

17

SIXTEEN little legs
were scaring the geese.

2 4 6 8 10 12 14 16

18

DIECISÉIS patitas
asustaban al ganso.

EIGHTEEN little legs
were scooped up by the
farmer's wife.

::	::	::	::	::	::	::	::	::
2	4	6	8	10	12	14	16	18

20

DIECIOCHO patitas recogió
la esposa del granjero.

TWENTY little legs were
back in the nest.

VEINTE patitas
regresaron al nido.

2 4 6 8 10 12 14 16 18 20

"Whew!" said Mrs. Hen. "These chicks really keep me on my toes!"

"¡Uf!" dijo la Sra. Gallina. "¡Estos pollitos sí que me mantienen ocupada!"

Fun Facts

- A hen lays an average of 300 eggs a year.

- There are more chickens in the world than people.

- The biggest chicken egg weighed more than 1 pound (.45 kilograms).

Find the Numbers

Now you have finished reading the story, but a surprise still awaits you. Hidden in each picture is a multiple of 2 from 2 to 20. Can you find them all?

2 – the hook above the door
4 – the handle of the shovel
6 – on the wheelbarrow wheel
8 – the pulley on the well
10 – on the tractor engine
12 – on the mud splash on the right page
14 – above the beans on the right page
16 – between the wings of the goose
18 – between the four eggs on the left
20 – on the bottom right eggshell

Internet Sites

FactHound offers a safe, fun way to find Internet sites related to this book. All of the sites on FactHound have been researched by our staff.
Here's all you do:
Visit *www.facthound.com*
Type in this code: 9781404862968

Datos divertidos

- Una gallina pone un promedio de 300 huevos al año.

- Hay más pollos que personas en el mundo.

- El huevo de pollo más grande pesó más de 1 libra (.45 kilogramos).

Encuentra los números

Ahora que ya terminaste de leer el cuento, aún te espera una sorpresa. En cada ilustración se encuentra escondido un múltiplo de 2, del 2 al 20. ¿Puedes encontrarlos a todos?

2 – el gancho arriba de la puerta
4 – el mango de la pala
6 – en la rueda de la carretilla
8 – en la polea del pozo
10 – en el motor del tractor
12 – en la mancha de barro en la página de la derecha
14 – sobre los frijoles en la página de la derecha
16 – entre las alas del ganso
18 – entre los cuatro huevos a la izquierda
20 – en el fondo del cascarón a la derecha

Sitios de Internet

FactHound brinda una forma segura y divertida de encontrar sitios de Internet relacionados con este libro. Todos los sitios en FactHound han sido investigados por nuestro personal.
Esto es todo lo que tienes que hacer:
Visita *www.facthound.com*
Ingresa este código: 9781404862968